CAREER EXPLORATION

in the Middle Grades

A PLAYBOOK FOR EDUCATORS

Copyright © by the Association for Middle Level Education. All rights reserved. No part of this publication may be reproduced or transmitted in any form or by any means, electronic or mechanical, without permission in writing from the publisher except in the case of brief quotations embodied in reviews or articles.

Printed in the United States of America.

This project is a collaboration between the Association for Middle Level Education and American Student Assistance® (ASA). Both organizations express gratitude to the team responsible for its publication:

Ashley Hemmy, M.Ed. Senior Program and Curriculum Specialist, ASA
Liliana Ornelas, M.Ed. Manager Programs & Curriculum, ASA
Avery Newton, Ph. D Educational Outcomes Research Manager, ASA
Alisa Wilke, MBA. VP Strategy & Innovation, ASA
Stephanie Simpson, J.D., CEO, AMLE
Derek Neal, CAE, COO, AMLE
Helen Polansky, Partnerships Coordinator, AMLE

Foreword by Nancy L. Deutsch, Ph.D.

ISBN: 9781737444305

Library of Congress Control Number: 2021941710

Table of Contents

	Foreword	v
1	**Why Career Exploration in Middle School?**	1
2	**Types of Programs and Best Practices**	7
	CASE STUDY: A Whole-School Approach Embedded in the Local Community	10
	CASE STUDY: A Whole-School Redesign with Students at the Center	14
	CASE STUDY: STEM Programming through a Dedicated Makerspace	18
	CASE STUDY: District-Level Implementation of PBL to Drive Student Exploration and Engagement	24
	CASE STUDY: Creating Engineering Exploration Opportunities with Student Choice at the Center	32
	CASE STUDY: Promoting Equity with a Bridge to STEM Program	36
3	**Program Planning and Implementation**	45

CASE STUDY: Using Family and Community   **51**
Engagement to Drive Program Success

CASE STUDY: Leveraging Community Connections   **55**
Through a Unified Approach

4   Program Assessment and Measurement   67

CASE STUDY: Leveraging Program Data, and a Student-   **69**
Centered Approach to Drive Program Success

5   Building a Community of Practice   79

CASE STUDY: The Launch Pad: A Career   **80**
Center Reimagined

Foreword

The middle grades are a time of tremendous change and transition for students. Their bodies are growing, their cognitive capacities are expanding, their social worlds are frequently in flux, and physiological and neurological changes are occurring in their brains and bodies at rates unseen since early childhood. All of this change can understandably leave both students and teachers feeling confused and sometimes frustrated. But these changes are also an incredible opportunity. When classrooms and curriculum are aligned with what young adolescents need, the middle grades are a time ripe for exploration, self-discovery, expanded learning, and thinking towards the future. This is what makes the Playbook so exciting.

The middle grades are, in general, the most under addressed period within the educational system, with fewer investments in the middle grades than in early childhood or the high school to post-secondary transition. In relation to career exploration, money and attention are focused on the end of the K-12 system, via high school graduation and college and career readiness. This is a missed opportunity. First, because the science is clear that the young adolescent years are critical and consequential, second only to early childhood in terms of the amount of developmental change and opportunity for growth. Second, because career exploration is distinctly aligned with the developmental tasks of early adolescence – the developmental period during which students are in the middle grades.

The middle grades are a natural time for self-exploration and self-directed learning. The concrete ideas presented here for how to infuse career exploration in both developmentally and academically meaningful ways are exciting for the opportunity they provide to transform the way educators approach schooling in the middle grades. Whereas educators sometimes associate career education as a narrower, vocational curriculum, this playbook highlights ASA's more expansive view of career exploration – an opening up of students' worlds rather than a narrowing into particular tracks.

This focus on exploration and thinking about possible future selves, varied interests, and an array of roles one can play in the world is precisely what young adolescents are seeking developmentally. By capitalizing on this and finding meaningful ways to integrate this exploration into both the academic curriculum and culture of the school, educators are creating middle grades structure and practices that should increase student engagement while also providing meaningful educational experiences.

This collaboration between ASA and AMLE is a critical and exciting project, because of the vision it represents. A vision in which we take young adolescents seriously not only as future high school students and citizens, but as current learners and explorers. The tools in this Playbook equip teachers to go beyond thinking about students in terms of their future labor market choices, although that is obviously important and is a foundation throughout the playbook. Yet by bringing the kind of career

Foreword

exploration represented here to their classrooms and schools, teachers will also be engaging students in answering the critical questions of youth: who am I and who do I want to be in the world, now and in the future?

Nancy L. Deutsch, Professor, University of Virginia School of Education and Human Development and Director of Youth-Nex: the UVA Center to Promote Effective Youth Development

Chapter 1

Why Career Exploration in Middle School?

Middle grades educators have the exciting opportunity to interact with students at a pivotal time in their development. Young adolescents are delightfully curious as they shift from concrete thinking to an increased capacity for abstract thinking. Their ability to engage in critical, analytical, and creative thinking grows, as does their desire to set personal goals and think about their own current and future needs.[1] During this time, students construct the attitudes, values, and dispositions that will form who they become as adults. They are excited and nervous as they think about life outside of high school.

Naturally, the middle grades are "the finding place" that invites young adolescents to be adventurous explorers. In order to nurture this, the general approach for the entire curriculum should be one of exploration. Career exploration is a cornerstone of this process. Educators have the power to equip students with the tools to help them discover their interests, try out new skills, and learn about future career and educational options.

Career exploration works; it is associated with both positive educational and employment outcomes, keeps students engaged in school, and helps them develop a better sense of self.[2] Extensive research supports middle school as the most effective time for career exploration. Notably, middle grades students are the most receptive to positive change following a career development intervention.[3] The formative years of middle school are especially critical to closing the achievement gap, increasing high school graduation rates, and improving college readiness. In particular, for students living in high-poverty areas, their middle-grade experience strongly impacts their likelihood of graduating from high school.[4]

Career exploration is a valuable tool that educators can use to increase student engagement. We know that student engagement sharply declines during the middle grades, with a majority of students reporting that their schoolwork is not engaging or worthwhile.[5] By providing experiences that help students learn about themselves and their future options, educators build connections throughout their content-specific lessons. There is also some evidence that career education is associated with improvements in self-efficacy, self-confidence, and decision-making skills.[6]

In addition to these broader benefits, we have found that the students themselves are invested in their own career development. Middle grades students are already thinking about the future and it is a primary source of stress. They desire guidance to help them uncover their interests and then match those interests with potential careers. According to American Student Assistance's nationally-representative survey of middle and high school students:

- Half of middle school students reported "picking the right career for me" as a source of stress;
- Forty-one percent reported "thinking about the future and what I will need to do to reach my future goals" as a source of stress;

Why Career Exploration in Middle School?

- Eighty-seven percent of middle school students are interested in ways to match their specific skills and interests with potential careers; and
- Eighty-five percent are interested in ways to learn the education and experience requirements needed for the careers they are interested in.[7]

Educators are preparing students for a labor market that is rapidly changing, especially due to technological innovation. Studies have shown that career education can be linked to positive economic and employment outcomes for youth and society at large.[8] Career education can be utilized to help students learn about what careers are projected to grow, how world events shape the careers of the future, and how their skills and interests can be used to catalyze change.

Overall, career exploration programming leads to increased student confidence, engagement, and academic growth. It brings relevance to what students are learning and provides the tools to help them make decisions about their futures. While the concept of purposeful career exploration is continually evolving, we know that strong programming extends beyond advisory blocks and career days into all parts of the school day. This type of exploration can be helpful for all students and should be neither a reward for high-achieving students nor a way to track students into specific careers. Every

> **This type of exploration can be helpful for all students and should be neither a reward for high-achieving students nor a way to track students into specific careers. Every student should be given the tools and opportunities to explore their future.**

student should be given the tools and opportunities to explore their future.

THE PLAYBOOK

American Student Assistance® (ASA) is a national non-profit with a mission of helping students know themselves, know their options, and make informed career and post-secondary education decisions. ASA's aim is to fuel a readiness revolution where every student leaves high school with a plan. ASA is devoted to shifting the conversion around career exploration: in school buildings, state houses, communities, and through direct-to-kid digital resources. Through a robust portfolio of middle school grant programming, research, and educational resources and products, ASA has developed a framework for career exploration best practices at the middle school level. Included in this grant programming is the ASA Middle School Career Exploration Grant, aimed at contributing to greater practices and programs that can be scaled or replicated anywhere. The findings from these school districts, who serve as thought leadership partners and incubators of innovation, contributed to ASA's learnings, the development of this playbook, and many of the case studies throughout. The Association for Middle Level Education (AMLE) is the largest international membership organization dedicated to helping middle school educators reach every student, grow professionally, and create great schools. With a community of more than 35,000 members strong, AMLE is the go-to source for peer-reviewed research, best practices, and professional development in the middle grades. Both organizations recognize the importance of providing impactful career exploration opportunities to young adolescents. ASA and AMLE have teamed up to create a playbook that equips educators with a roadmap for creating effective career exploration programming. You will find helpful resources like implementation guides, case studies, and program sustainability resources.

The programs described in this playbook offer students an opportunity to recognize their strengths and interests, gain awareness of different career pathways, and help them better understand labor market trends and future opportunities. We provide the beginning framework for many types of programs, as well as the tools to scale programming into other areas of the school and district. The playbook has a role for everyone on the middle school team: administrators, counselors, and teachers can all enact purposeful, engaging career exploration programming in a variety of ways. We also provide strategies and recommendations for how to build a community of practice that involves all stakeholders in career exploration work: students, educators, families, and community members.

Effective career exploration is a comprehensive process that involves shifting school culture. This playbook will serve as a guide to help you map your journey from beginning initiatives to school-wide practice. And it is a journey worth undertaking, as studies have shown that career education positively impacts K–12 students decades later. When engaging in the career exploration programming described in this playbook, educators are providing opportunities for students to dream about their futures and imagine the possibilities.

Be sure to utilize the accompanying online Resource Center for the most updated information and tools.

amle.org/playbook

NOTES

[1] Bishop, P.A. & Harrison, L.M. (2021). *The successful middle school: This we believe.* Association for Middle Level Education.

[2] Association for Career and Technical Education (ACTE). (2017). Career exploration in middle school: Setting students on the path to success. Alexandria, VA: ACTE and Career Cruising. Retrieved on February 25,2020 from https://www.acteonline.org/wp-content/uploads/2018/02/ACTE_CC_Paper_FINAL.pdf

[3] Whiston, S. C., Rossier, J., & Hernandez Barón, P. M. (2017). Evidence Based Practice in Career and Workforce Development Interventions. The Handbook of Career and Workforce Development Research, Practice, and Policy, 39–56.

[4] Balfanz, R. (2009). Putting Middle Grades Students on the Graduation Path: A Policy and Practice Brief. Baltimore, MD: Everyone Graduates Center at Johns Hopkins University, Philadelphia Education Fund, and National Middle School Association. Retrieved on February 25, 2020 from https://www.amle.org/portals/0/pdf/articles/policy_brief_balfanz.pdf

[5] TNTP. (2018). Opportunity Myth: What Students Can Show Us About How School is Letting Them Down – and How to Fix It. Retrieved on March 2, 2020 from file:///Users/dansel/Documents/TNTP_The-Opportunity-Myth_Web.pdf

[6] Hughes, D, et al. (2016). Careers education: International Literature Review. London, England: Education Endowment Foundation. Retrieved on March 5, 2020 from https://www.educationandemployers.org/wp-content/uploads/2016/07/Careers-review.pdf

[7] American Student Assistance. (2018). Survey of 2,393 middle and high school students in the United States, December 2018.

[8] Hughes, D, et al. (2016). Careers education: International Literature Review. London, England: Education Endowment Foundation. Retrieved on March 5, 2020 from https://www.educationandemployers.org/wp-content/uploads/2016/07/Careers-review.pdf

Chapter 2

Types of Programs and Best Practices

While all career exploration programming focuses on similar objectives—helping middle schoolers learn about their interests and future options—implementation looks vastly different in each school. This should be expected, since the most impactful programs are tailored to student interests/skills and are built with the surrounding community in mind.

With sustainability in mind, programming should be planned longitudinally by a collaborative, multi-disciplinary team. Setting measurable, attainable goals is pivotal for first-year success, while also strategizing for the next three to five years to ensure program longevity. To accomplish these goals, schools should build a community of practice that involves everyone in the school building in partnership with families and the surrounding community. When all stakeholders are involved, career exploration evolves from stand-alone activities to embedded, purposeful daily work.

This chapter provides a thorough list of documented best practices, yet it is incomplete. New initiatives and programs launch each year, and our understanding of middle school career exploration continues to grow. As new technological advancements and an ever-changing labor market shift the shape of future careers, career exploration in education also evolves. Be sure to check the accompanying online Resource Center at **https://www.amle.org/playbook** for the most updated information and tools.

TYPES OF CAREER EXPLORATION PROGRAMMING

Most career exploration programming falls under three categories: whole-school implementation, counseling-centered programming, and Science Technology Engineering and Math (STEM) or STEAM (adds Arts) programs. Programs that fit in these three groupings typically feature practices such as work-based learning and project-based learning, though these can also be utilized as frameworks for stand-alone career exploration programming.

Whole-School Program Implementation

Many strong career exploration programs are built in a whole-school model, where exposing students to future options becomes part of the school's mission and daily routine. Building a community of practice is at the core of this model, with all school stakeholders involved in planning and implementation. The methods and practices of whole-school program implementation can vary, but usually include:

> Many strong career exploration programs are built in a whole-school model, where exposing students to future options becomes part of the school's mission and daily routine.

- **School Culture Shift**: The school/district shifts the mission and entire culture to prioritize career exploration. School leaders adapt schedules to ensure all students can access programming. Professional development that focuses on career exploration programming is prioritized and cross-curricular units and projects planned by all stakeholders are common practice.
- **School-Wide Events**: Programming focuses on events

and initiatives attended by all students and staff, such as assemblies, career days, and project showcases. School staff collaborate to plan and execute events.
- **Pathways-Focused**: Schools may create pathways in its course offerings to provide more focused exploration opportunities for students. Students select from different electives, or exploratory choices may be provided within core content areas.
- **Middle and High School Transitions**: Some districts have robust Career and Technical Education (CTE) programs, and the middle and high schools collaborate so the middle school operates as a bridge to those high school programs. Other times, the middle and high schools may collaborate to link the programs through transition planning. Bridging middle and high school programs has many benefits for students as they are provided with more opportunities to explore and build on their employability skills. The district may benefit as well, whether it be positive academic impact or, for districts where students apply to a high school of choice, maintaining a curriculum that motivates students to stay in their pipeline.

CASE STUDY: A Whole-School Approach Embedded in the Local Community

Uxbridge High School, Uxbridge, Massachusetts

Uxbridge High School (UHS) is a grade 8–12 comprehensive high school of approximately 600 students located in central Massachusetts. The centerpiece of the community is a new building that includes several multipurpose areas and lab spaces ideal for authentic and applied learning. Eighth grade was brought to the UHS campus in 2018, thereby expanding these students' access to our robust elective program.

This elective program enables students to graduate from Uxbridge High School with access to industry-recognized credentials and technical training, advanced academic coursework, and a guided academic pathway that supports postsecondary decision-making. The school revamped its counseling program to align with a five-year model that enables students to make purposeful decisions about their futures, and students in 8th grade participate in an exploratory model that provides exposure to all of UHS' pathways. As of spring 2021, the following pathways have been approved:

- Media/Information Science
- Biomedical Science
- Manufacturing/Engineering
- Business, Finance, and Logistics

Several factors drove the development of these pathways. Primarily, the number of UHS students that had historically applied to the local vocational technical high school far exceeded the number of accepted students. Additionally, for approximately 20 percent of graduates, plans for postsecondary experiences included either a two-year/technical program or immediate employment. By partnering with local industry, we were able to align the programs we developed with local economic needs. The school administration and school council collaborate with the local Chamber of Commerce, the Central Massachusetts Workforce Investment Board (MassHire), and the Commonwealth of Massachusetts to merge community supply and demand with schools.

Because 8th grade is part of the UHS community, the skills—both technical and essential/soft—are consistent and evaluated through the lens of postsecondary outcomes. Using grant funds from the Commonwealth, Uxbridge offers students access to industry-standard equipment. Students are trained on CNC routers, laser engravers, unmanned aircraft (drones), anatomy tables, and 3D printing.

Moving forward, UHS continues to take steps to minimize attrition. In the early days, 8th grade students could enroll in courses without prerequisite knowledge. The implementation of career pathways has helped drive better academic outcomes, particularly as students examine the connection between their interests, general course of study, and selected pathway. Similarly, families feel better prepared to support students in the college and career decision-making process. Similarly, with students starting earlier the decision-making process for families around interests and credentials has supported a better and more thorough analysis of college and career readiness. In the long-term, students will gain a more comprehensive familiarity with postsecondary and career pathways, which will, in turn, drive improved access, decision-making, and success.

Key factors to our success have included:

- Examining the nexus between the school and local economic trends to both identify workforce partners and drive relevant curricular adaptations.
- Using data, recommendations, and insights to drive staff development, training, and technology deployment.

- Providing school counselors, students, parents, and other relevant stakeholders with consistent communication so they have a specific understanding of the curricular purpose of these courses.
- Promoting flexibility among school leadership with outcomes, staffing, and scheduling needs. The development of these programs is not an exercise in immediate impact, and the third year of the program will no doubt look different than the first.

Michael D. Rubin, Principal of Uxbridge High School

CASE STUDY: A Whole-School Redesign with Students at the Center

Barnstable Intermediate School, Hyannis, Massachusetts

Barnstable Intermediate School (BIS) is a grade 6–7 urban public school. Our student population of more than 700 is racially and economically diverse. BIS embarked on its journey to include a career exploratory experience as part of a larger whole-school redesign tasked with bringing rigorous, relevant, and engaged learning to all students while building on school-based, family, and community relationships. We obtained funding from ASA and Mass IDEAS to support this work.

BIS leverages monthly half days for students to begin their career exploratory experience. The goal of these half days is to lead students through a discovery phase of career exploration that supports them to identify their skills, passions, and talents, while also exposing them to available opportunities as they progress through their secondary education and beyond. Students engage with individual guest speakers to build upon work happening in the classrooms, explore a variety of local career opportunities, and participate in a whole-school Career Day.

A strong relationship was built between BIS and Barnstable High School (BHS) to ensure the continuity of career exploration from grades 6 through 12. High School Career Ambassadors were established to introduce 6th and 7th grade students to the high school pathways, internships, and other opportunities in their near future.

The results of this work were evident as 126 of the 358 6th grade students showed interest in taking part in a new 7th grade elective, Pathfinder, that was developed to provide a deeper dive into career exploration during the following school year. Additionally, through the work with the Career Ambassadors, the majority of 7th grade teachers reported that students had thoughtfully investigated and selected 8th grade courses with the 9 career pathways at BHS in mind.

BIS is continuing its work to bring a robust career exploratory experience to its students by expanding the Pathfinder elective, providing week-long career exploratory experiences held monthly in small group advisories, and hosting weekly spotlights of community members who share their journeys to their current careers with BIS students. BIS's vision for career explorations has grown over the last two years and its commitment to create rigorous, relevant, and engaging learning experiences, including career exploration, has deepened as a result of the impact the programming has had on our students' engagement and ownership of their learning.

Key Insights:

- It was extremely important to share a clear message with families, students, and the community that career exploration at the middle school level is not having students select a path for their future; rather, career exploration in middle school provides students an opportunity to make their learning relevant as they explore connections to careers and, ultimately, may open doors to their future through exploring their skills, passions, and talents early on in their educational journeys.
- Developing a whole-school career exploration experience takes time, focus, and community-wide effort. Time needs to be given to educators to help them understand

the importance of the work, curate lessons, and build relationships with community members.
- Lean on your staff to jump-start your community relationship building. We initially asked educators to contribute their local contacts to a list of potential partnerships we could build upon as a school. By using our educators' established relationships, we were able to skip the cold call step of building local partnerships for our school.
- Creating roles responsible for this work is key. Establishing a Career Exploration Liaison and subcommittee brought focus to our work and supported the development of lessons in order to create consistency during the early phases.

Julie DiPilato, Grants Project Manager, and Jen Perry, Director of Teaching and Learning, 6–12

Counseling-Centered Implementation

A guidance counselor's role typically includes career and education planning, but ASA research indicates most counselors can only devote 7 percent of their time to it. Developing a counselor-centered program is one method for counselors to extend their expertise to other staff members and students. Some examples of counselor-centered career exploration programs are:

- **Counselor-Led Planning and Professional Development:** Counselors may collaborate with teachers to develop a career readiness curriculum or create one themselves and train teachers to implement it in their classrooms. In order to establish effective counselor-led planning, it is crucial for

the counselor to have strong relationships with teachers and continually work to build staff buy-in.
- **Advisory Blocks or Innovation Centers:** Some counselors teach students during an advisory block devoted to career exploration. In other schools, a classroom is set aside as an innovation center that students can visit throughout the day, or during extracurriculars or specific electives to learn about career options.
- **Guidance-Focused Programs or Products**: Some districts invest in a counseling-based program or product that staff can use throughout the year. Many digital programs launch yearly and provide useful tools for instruction that require little prep for educators.
- **Small-Group Learning:** Counselors may have small groups of students they pull throughout the week, or they may push into specific classrooms. Targeted instruction helps guide students based on their specific interests or needs. While this method leads to large individual impact, it can be difficult to scale to all students in the building.

STEM/STEAM Programs

STEM (Science, Technology, Engineering, and Math) and STEAM (includes Art) programs have been increasing in popularity. There is a greater need for young adults to be skilled in these fields due to a massive shift toward technology-focused jobs in the labor market. STEM and STEAM programs provide dynamic, engaging ways for students to explore possible skills and careers. Some STEM or STEAM programs include:
- **Class Offerings:** STEM or STEAM is sometimes offered as an elective or required course. Multiple STEM/STEAM courses can be offered to provide students with a wide

array of experiences; coding, robotics, and 3D printing are examples of middle school course offerings we support.
- **Innovation or STEM/STEAM Labs:** Some schools establish a space devoted to STEM/STEAM exploration; labs that hold makerspaces, technology, and student projects become the site for classrooms and extracurricular clubs to imagine and create.
- **STEM/STEAM Events:** School-wide events devoted to STEM/STEAM are useful ways to engage multiple stakeholders in student learning. Some event options include STEM/STEAM nights, project showcases, career days, or school-wide contests and bootcamps.

CASE STUDY: STEM Programming through a Dedicated Makerspace

Miscoe Hill Middle School, Mendon, Massachusetts

The Miscoe Hill Middle School (MA) Inspired Innovation Center (IIC) opened in 2019. The IIC's purpose is to offer career-exploration learning via a school-wide maker program. The IIC is a makerspace where students engage in hands-on, curriculum- or interest-oriented learning that yields meaningful products.

We developed the vision IIC in consultation with national experts in maker education, including Sylvia Martinez, Mike Stone, Pam Moran, and Ira Socol. We then sought input from students, faculty, and families. Our vision evolves with the emerging interests and needs of our school community.

We have learned a great deal since opening, but our most significant learning concerns the usage of space. Initially, the IIC was the home for our grade 5 technology courses. The makerspace was an ideal location to launch our new Project Lead the Way (PLTW) Design & Modeling course. Design & Modeling fostered hands-on, real-world, problem-oriented learning through prototyping. Students had an outstanding experience and the course is a mainstay in our technology curriculum.

However, we found that running a class in the makerspace presented additional challenges. Given our schedule, IIC was being used as a technology classroom for four of the six blocks. As a result, general curriculum teachers had a hard time envisioning rotating their own four classes through the IIC for projects when the technology course would also be in the room for two overlapping sessions. Even though the room could accommodate multiple classes, teachers expressed concern about "encroaching" on a colleague's classroom. So, while the IIC was actively used in year one, the impact was limited to just the technology course.

To expand access to the IIC, we shifted the technology course to a new location and reframed the Innovation Center as an "open lab." Teachers schedule time to bring their classes, and students are able to use the space on an ad hoc basis for video recording or 3D printing projects for classes. As we expand our PLTW programming, we will use the Innovation Center for specific projects or lessons, but the space will not be assigned to a particular course or teacher.

The open lab is not without its challenges. We are still working on revising our curricular units to leverage Innovation Center resources, so the IIC is not used as frequently. Additionally, an open lab structure benefits from having a dedicated staff member who would manage the facility, provide access and training to students, and reach out to colleagues to initiate projects. Currently we have distributed these responsibilities across different staff members, which is suboptimal given the other demands on their time. Despite these limitations, we are making excellent progress.

In the big picture, we believe that the open lab provides the largest possibility for impact as compared to a single course. However, we continue to reflect on our decisions, analyze the outcomes, and adjust course where necessary so we may further revise our structure. And the vision evolves with time and experience. As we have worked to increase access to and use of the Inspired Innovation Center, we have found several approaches that have served us well:

1. **Set a Trap: Feed 'em:** While some colleagues will naturally gravitate to your new makerspace, many may not due to a lack of knowledge. When we opened the IIC in the fall of 2019, we held a breakfast for all staff members and had the new resources out and available for people to see and touch. We had our 3D printer running so staff could see it in action. And we also posted two questions on the white boards and asked staff for feedback to help our planning. We asked:
    a. How might you use some of these resources in your curriculum?
    b. What's missing that we can add to the IIC?

2. **Focus on the End User:** Your colleagues may be slow to jump on board, but many students will be itching to "make." Ask them about the resources they need and provide them with dedicated time to access the space. At Miscoe Hill we are working on developing training

modules for the different tools we have in the Innovation Center. We believe that the modules will both build student capacity while also sparking ideas for products they can make in future curricular projects. Additionally, teacher apprehension to maker-oriented learning may be reduced when trained students can serve as "peer experts" on how to use the 3D printer or laser cutter, etc.

3. **Don't Be Afraid to Ask:** Industry professionals are surprisingly eager to "give back" to schools. Given the propensity of video conferencing, it's easier than ever to bring the community to your classroom. External partners are great at consulting on your project's design, giving an opening "kick-off" presentation, or providing authentic feedback on student work. We use industry connector tools such as ASA Engage/Nepris to connect our students with experts across the country.

4. **Invite Families to Become Co-Makers:** Offering maker events for families is a fantastic way to build student capacity and family support for your program. Prior to the pandemic, we offered monthly in-person workshops on 3D printing and robotics. This year we've continued the workshops virtually. We've focused on the micro:bit "do your :bit" challenge because of the small size and low cost of the materials yielded. Be sure to emphasize the collaborative nature of the events and the importance of adult participation.

5. **Provide Updates at Faculty Meetings:** Ask your building principal for two minutes (brevity is essential) at the faculty meeting's beginning, while attention is still

fresh. Use your time to showcase a new product that students can create in the makerspace and invite colleagues to collaborate.
6. **Find the Others:** Innovation is a team sport. While this work can feel lonely, others across the country and globe are engaged in this work. Twitter is an excellent platform for Finding the Others.

These are just a few of the many strategies that can help build a deeply engaged culture. Not all of them will apply to your context. Regardless of your method, we would encourage you to "play the long game" and adopt a persistence and reflection mindset. Your program's vision will evolve as you learn from mistakes and encounter opportunities that only present themselves in time. Patience is a virtue and is also the key to flourishing career exploration programming.

Dave Quinn, Directory of Technology Integration

Work-Based Learning

Work-based learning is utilized across career exploration programming models, but it is also useful as a stand-alone practice. This instructional method is experiential-focused; students engage in hands-on activities in an authentic setting that draws on their academic, technical, and employability skills.[1] Some work-based learning practices include:

- **Experiential Learning**: Authentic, real-world experiences provide students opportunities to explore careers and test out their interests and skills. At the middle school level, experiential opportunities could include field trips,

job shadowing, volunteering, apprenticeships, digital simulations, and credentials-based learning.
- **Alignment of Classroom Standards to Employability Skills:** Work-based learning does not necessarily occur outside the classroom. Exposing students to classroom activities that utilize emotional, technical, and academic skills relevant to the workplace can also set them up for success. Case studies or challenges provide opportunities for students to tackle and reflect on real-world problems. Students can practice digital literacy skills across subject areas, and career inventories and portfolios can also be used to expand learning.
- **Connecting with Industry Professionals**: Collaborating with industry professionals offers exciting opportunities for students to connect with people currently working in the field. Invited professionals can participate in career days, student mentorships, and project showcases. Developing a portfolio of professionals from different fields is an important component of building a community of practice that extends beyond the school walls.

Project-Based Learning

Through the use of long-range, cross-curricular projects, project-based learning (PBL) employs goal setting, problem-solving, twenty-first century learning, and many other skills to prepare students for postsecondary success. PBL can be utilized in all career exploration implementation models as well as in singular classrooms within a building. Importantly, PBL is a valuable resource for embedding career exploration in any content area, including English Language, Arts, and Social Studies. The core components of PBL[2] make it a long-standing part of middle school career exploration:

- **Tackling a Driving Question**: Projects focus on a driving question, which tasks students with researching and exploring a topic in-depth to develop multiple solutions to the same problem. Honing in on a driving question challenges students to set specific project goals and cultivate knowledge to make connections, understand different perspectives, and collaborate with peers.
- **Reflection and Feedback**: Students are expected to self-assess, reflect, and determine next steps. PBL is action-oriented, so students take risks and learn to acknowledge and reassess when mistakes occur. These are crucial skills that benefit students academically while also preparing them for the future. Both teachers and peers provide feedback throughout the process, which helps students learn to take feedback constructively to advance their project.
- **Presenting to an Authentic Audience**: While developing their solutions to their driving questions, students also create artifacts to present to an audience. Most PBL units culminate in a project showcase, which involves student presentations to their peers, families, educators, and community members.

CASE STUDY: District-Level Implementation of PBL to Drive Student Exploration and Engagement

Broward County Public Schools, Broward County, Florida

With a keen focus on the experience for the middle school students, Reimagining Middle Grades officially launched in Broward County Public Schools in July 2018. Commitment to impacting the pivotal middle grades years was amplified with the support from stakeholders like the Community Foundation of Broward, who partnered with the Broward Schools in offering the largest grant in their history.

Through intentional incorporation of project-based learning and social-emotional instruction, we believe that on-grade-level performance will improve in English Language, Arts, and Math, and that students will successfully transition to high school and beyond. The key levers in Reimagining Middle Grades have been:

1. Exposure to more project-based learning experiences in the classroom;
2. Creation of a warm supportive environment where students' educational needs are met;
3. Expanded opportunities for elective offerings; and
4. Connection to extracurricular opportunities, such as clubs or sports.

With 44 different schools servicing middle grades students, we strategically divided some schools to have a focus in the project-based learning implementation model and others to have a focus on social-emotional learning. Twenty-five schools have participated in the project-based learning (PBL) implementation model.

To establish understanding and a common language about PBL, we have partnered with PBL Works to offer the professional opportunities to our teachers. Administrators have also spent time articulating their vision for PBL, creating capacity their building, sustaining the work, and crafting the culture that fosters immersive and connected learning opportunities where students are able to express themselves in meaningful ways. The initial step includes the principal along with the leadership team and key teacher leaders, who together give shape to the focus and approach for the project-based learning experience. The individual teams then receive planning time to determine their driving question, standards, calendar of events, project milestones, and public products.

Part of this learning is evidenced through presentations that show how learning is connected and relevant. These showcase a culmination of student learning and include audiences of peers, parents, and field experts (such as community members or business leaders) who bring a different level of critique to the student work. By making the product public, students will naturally want to revisit their product throughout the process to make sure their final presentation is truly the most polished version. These presentations of learning have occurred face-to-face and continued virtually.

Below is an example of one of our schools, Margate Middle School, which has integrated career exploration and project-based learning:

- Students visit Junior Achievement, allowing them to develop a profile to determine their areas of interest and create plans for their future.
- A partnership with Nepris provides students with exposure to a variety of careers through engagement with professionals, including health and medical experts.
- The current realities of the pandemic have catapulted the inclusion of PBL as a school-wide practice at Margate Middle. Teachers have stepped outside of their normal mode of instruction to embrace PBL at a larger scale. This

expansion naturally lent itself to collaboration among the teachers and the continuation of structures, such as a monthly professional learning community for PBL. Project-based learning experiences have even been incorporated into the extended learning opportunities offered through the Enrichment Spring Break Camp. Margate Middle believes that as a result of this pandemic, more teachers have embraced technology platforms and are taking their instruction to the next level.

Project-based learning naturally lends itself to the inclusion of outside experts. The principal, leadership team, and key teacher leaders help determine the focus and approach for the project-based learning experience, with input provided by other teachers as well. From that point, the teams then collaborate to bring the PBL to life. The role of the field experts allows for them to offer insights to students on the topic, critique student work, and even be authentic audience members for the students as they present their final product.

Here are some lessons and key insights we have learned along the way:

- The thought that PBL experiences should be offered primarily to high-achieving students has been challenged and now PBL is offered to all students. The results affirm that learning should not be limited to pockets of students; with the proper scaffolds, all students can experience success.
- Social-emotional learning has been incorporated along

with key literature pieces to integrate relevant social issues and address trauma from the pandemic.
- Teachers continue to refine their practice and each time, the implementation gets better. Teachers continue to deepen their learning in PBL, consider how to create standards-aligned rubrics, and define clear student outcomes.
- Teacher buy-in is an issue, along with the abundance of standards available to teachers which can be overwhelming and too broad in nature. Time is a factor and many teachers believe that PBLs are lengthy in nature. The reality is that the experience to be created can be as short or extensive as desired.
- To address teacher buy-in concerns, Margate would like to strategically partner teachers by their comfort level in PBL so that there is collegial guidance and the team stays on course. The school hopes to continue offering opportunities for career tie-ins and Nepris will be a big part of that.

Career exploration has broadened the perspective of our students, as they are now able to learn about fields they did not know previously existed. When you enter a classroom and observe students learning from a field expert, you can see the WOW in their eyes. Shifting to project-based learning with a focus on career exploration is a process. It requires patience and the baby steps must be honored. The reward will be greater when you let things take their course.

Tanya Thompson, Project Coordinator, Re-Imagining Middle Grades, Broward County Public Schools

MIDDLE SCHOOL CAREER EXPLORATION BEST PRACTICES

Whole-school implementation, counseling-centered programs, and STEM/STEAM programs, whether engaging in work-based learning, project-based learning, or other relevant practices, can be developed into sustaining, dynamic middle school career exploration programs. The most impactful programs can all be characterized as:

- Exploratory
- Student-centered
- Innovative
- Inclusive and equitable
- Built around twenty-first century skills
- Supported by a community of practice
- Sustainable and scalable
- Informed by outcomes and feedback to drive progress

Exploratory

While middle school is the best time for students to begin learning about career options, it is not the time for them to make final decisions about their futures. Instead, students should have space to explore, consider, and try as many skills and interests as they can. It is just as important for students to discover what they dislike as what they like. This is about opening doors, not closing them; a greater understanding of their identity will serve them well when making future choices.

This need for exploration is supported by ASA research which found that half of all middle schoolers feel none of the careers they are aware of appeal to them. Furthermore, one in three felt they were not familiar enough with their skills and interests to even begin thinking of a career. But, overall, they are very interested in learning what is out there:

- Sixty-six percent enjoy exploring and thinking about what their future career might look like;
- Seventy-five percent are interested in learning about what careers they are best suited for;
- Eighty-seven percent are interested in ways to match their specific skills and interest with careers; and
- Eighty-seven percent are interested in learning about different careers that may interest them.[3]

The need for programming that is exploratory is beneficial for all middle grades students, but especially first-generation students and students of color who may have less exposure to the range of career possibilities available to them. Educators should provide opportunities for students to learn about careers they may not yet be familiar with and to imagine what the job market could look like when they reach adulthood.

> **The need for programming that is exploratory is beneficial for all middle grades students, but especially first-generation students and students of color who may have less exposure to the range of career possibilities available to them.**

Exploratory learning also involves experimenting with different skill sets. Students should be provided varied opportunities to develop skills, including classroom activities that involve writing, building, planning, and creating. When a project focuses on a skill that a student enjoys and feels confident with, they should be encouraged to explore professional pathways that utilize those skills. Students can dream bigger when they have the opportunity to expand their awareness of all the options that exist for them.

Student-Centered

Instruction that is student-centered increases critical thinking, engagement, and interest in academic content; and this is especially true for STEM- and STEAM-based classrooms.[4] When students are active participants in their learning, they feel more empowered to try new things and take risks.

Programming should not just be based on student interests, but should also be developmentally appropriate. Young adolescent learners typically prefer hands-on activities, teamwork, and experiences based on real-world scenarios.[5] Educators should consider the whole child, embrace individuality, and differentiate by students' learning styles. They can do this by incorporating choice in educational activities (through student menus and other choice-based activities), exposing students to careers in many different fields, and providing opportunities for students to select topics to explore. This increases student responsibility, independence, creativity, and ownership of their work.[6]

Work-based and project-based learning practices specifically contribute to developing a student-centered program. Some student-centered, work-based learning practices include career inventories, individualized student career plans, and student portfolios. During a project-based learning unit, students may be challenged to develop their own topics or driving questions, decide on potential solutions, and determine how to showcase their learning.

CASE STUDY: Creating Engineering Exploration Opportunities with Student Choice at the Center

Sutton Middle School, Sutton, Massachusetts

Our career exploration journey began when a district-wide Vision Committee composed of parents, educators, students, and school committee members determined more engineering opportunities were needed for our students. Our principal applied for a grant from ASA, which allowed us to develop the following 45-day mini-electives in the 8th grade to give students a taste of different engineering skill sets and careers:

- 3D Modeling and Printing;
- Sports Engineering (collaboration with the gym teacher);
- Green Engineering; and
- Helper Engineering.

In our first year of programming, students were thrilled to have some choice! While remote learning limited our ability to offer these mini-electives in the second year, it presented the opportunity to pivot to create a new class: Design Thinking Product Development. Students spent the first few months learning the design thinking process and doing hands-on projects with different STEM kits. Students built confidence while becoming familiar with various prototyping materials, then applied design thinking to develop a new product:

1. They chose to work individually or in small groups.
2. They chose the population for which they wanted to design, conducted interviews, established goals for this

population, and then designed a product that helped the population meet one of their goals.
3. They built a prototype, received additional feedback from the population, and then created a business and marketing plan for the product.
4. Finally, they gave a Shark Tank-style presentation. We were fortunate to have professionals from a variety of fields Zoom into our class to listen to the student presentations and give feedback and encouragement.

Some of our lessons learned include:

- Design lessons for the students in front of you! Give opportunities for various talents to shine; and give lots of choice. When students were "stuck" and couldn't think of what to make, I encouraged them to follow their passions, or what they most liked to do.
- For career-minded lessons, try to incorporate "real-world" activities as much as possible. While these activities may be above their capabilities, you may also be surprised by how much they can do. By conducting research on how similar products were made, some students learned much more about manufacturing than I thought they might.
- Low-fidelity prototypes are perfectly acceptable. Students were able to make prototypes of their designs, many of which were made of cardboard and tape. If you don't have a 3D printer, students can design prototypes with Tinkercad and can even share their prototypes by screen sharing the Tinkercad file and rotating the view from different angles.
- This course gave students the opportunity to develop

skills such as coding, 3D modeling, circuit design, prototyping, determining a product's price, logo development, package design, and public speaking, while exposing them to fields such as engineering, business, marketing, and entrepreneurship. Next year, we will return to giving students choice in their electives, but an additional elective will be offered: Shark Tank.

Vanessa Haerle, STEM Teacher

Innovative

By middle school, students have developed a greater capacity for considering their futures, and they are interested in learning through engaging, hands-on activities.[7] Innovative, out-of-the-box activities and novel opportunities to learn and create can provide students with exciting opportunities to try different skills. Providing access to emerging technologies, such as 3D printers, drones, and STEM kits, can also facilitate important learning experiences for students while helping them understand what skills might be required for future jobs.[8] Creating a makerspace prioritizes ways for students to build and learn creatively.

With that said, innovation in middle school career exploration must extend beyond offering access to the latest tech tools. Innovation includes embracing different approaches to education, adapting the school-wide schedule to prioritize student-centered instruction, setting aside time for educators to collaborate across content areas to create authentic learning experiences for students, and developing new electives to build pathways for students. By allowing innovation in pedagogical practices, schools and districts can implement a program that is accessible and engaging for students and educators alike.

Inclusive and Equitable

Career exploration has value for all students. Opportunities to learn and explore their many possible futures is especially important for economically disadvantaged students, students of color, female students, and first-generation students.[9]

Career exploration has been shown to increase engagement, which in turn drives attendance, academic performance, and positive classroom behaviors—all crucial to closing the achievement gap.[10] Some challenges to equitable access to career exploration programming include availability of industry resources and professionals in different geographic areas, access to information for families, and access to counseling resources.[11]

To address these challenges, school districts must commit to investing funds in programming, finding creative ways to expose students to diverse careers and professionals, and expanding access to all postsecondary educational pathways.[12] Districts can increase the reach of programs by engaging families as assets in career exploration, bridging programs to support student transitions throughout their secondary education, and experimenting with middle school-level CTE programs.[13] To bridge geographical challenges, schools/districts can utilize digital resources to provide experiences and access to professionals when they are not locally available.

All students deserve the opportunity to plan for their futures, and schools can make this happen by prioritizing career exploration programming and proactively addressing challenges to program equity.

CASE STUDY: Promoting Equity with a Bridge to STEM Program

Charlotte-Mecklenburg Schools, Charlotte, North Carolina

As a middle grades science educator at a Title 1 school, I have had to overcome many challenges to implement career exploration in my classroom. A strategy I have developed is to expose my students to STEM career opportunities. With 99.4 percent of my students eligible for free or reduced lunch, it is essential they are aware of career choices that can help them raise their socioeconomic status.

Changing the economic outlook of my students was the inspiration of the Bridge to STEM program at my school. Programming takes place after school and infuses field trips, guest speakers, and online instruction to expose middle grades students to careers in STEM fields that do not require a four-year degree. Bridge to STEM program is a collaborative effort between my school and several community partners. The role of these partners is to support the students with guest speakers and field trip opportunities, and to provide volunteers to assist with PBL assignments. Bridge to STEM is a relatively new program, but students have already been able to gain insight into computer coding careers, robotics, aviation, and machining/manufacturing careers.

The program came to fruition when I received the endorsement from my principal. With her approval, I reached out to community partners I worked with in the past to ask if they were interested in assisting with a program that exposes students to STEM careers. With an overwhelmingly positive response, we began setting up meetings.

After this year's pilot of the program, our survey data found that students who participated in the program self-identified as a potential STEM worker. For example, when asked what a person in STEM looks like, one 7th grade girl responded, "Black, Brown, White...any color or race." Another 7th grade girl responded, "I see STEM workers as women." These examples help reveal the importance of programs such as Bridge to STEM.

Programs like Bridge to STEM are an essential part of middle school instruction especially in historically marginalized communities. Students should be able to make the connections between what they are learning and its relevant to career opportunities. With this insight they can begin to have career aspirations they once thought were unobtainable, and change the negative perceptions that can sometimes be associated with

> STEM instruction. We recently obtained a grant from a community partner to provide funding for the next five years, and I can't wait to see where it takes us next!
>
> **W. Keith Burgess, Science Teacher**

Built Around Twenty-First Century Skills

Career exploration is more than exposure to careers; it is also about developing the skills necessary for postsecondary success. Embedding twenty-first century skill development provides students with opportunities to grow as individuals, teammates, and members of their school community. It is also positively correlated to problem solving, self-directed learning capabilities, overcoming adversities, and goal setting.[14] Twenty-first century skills include collaboration, communication, problem solving, creativity, adaptability, and technology usage. Studies show that employer's value these skills, and strong twenty-first century skill development leads to academic success as well as improved employment outcomes.[15]

Students must both understand what twenty-first century skills are and practice these skills in varied situations.[16] Educators should provide frequent opportunities for students to connect, communicate, and collaborate with each other, adapt projects to include problem solving and chances to express creativity, and integrate a range of digital tools into student projects. By engaging students in twenty-first century skills, educators can help prepare students for success in whatever career they choose.

Supported by a Community of Practice

Based on observations of the school districts ASA supports, we concluded that the strongest indicator of programmatic success is building a community of practice around career exploration.

Building a sustainable program involves engaging all stakeholders: school and district leaders, counselors, teachers, members of the community, and families. When all stakeholders collaborate to provide authentic educational experiences, students are engaged by multiple touchpoints and have a greater chance of understanding the content. This topic is so important we have dedicated the concluding chapter 5 to exploring this concept in more detail.

Sustainable and Scalable

Program sustainability is often linked with access to funding, which can be especially difficult to obtain at the middle school level. Without adequate funding, program implementation and sustainability may seem an impossible feat. The Playbook's online Resource Center provides detailed guides and resources to obtaining funding for your program.

Developing a program that continues beyond the initial year involves much more than funding. Critical elements include creating a comprehensive plan that sets measurable short- and long-term goals, scales programming over time, includes staff training and buy-in, and builds a community of practice. Programmatic sustainability is a process, and one that should be scaffolded over a number of years. Focusing on a few measurable goals is a critical step during that initial year of programming; adding too many products, training, or activities all at once can overburden staff.[17]

Informed by Outcomes and Feedback to Drive Progress

Targeted program evaluation can be used to drive progress when embedded in everyday work. Along with goal setting, schools should determine what to measure and begin to collect data on programmatic outcomes. What will a successful program look like? What are measures of student success? How will outcomes inform future decisions? These questions not only drive goal setting but could also inform implementation decisions about what educational products to utilize or in which classrooms to pilot programming.

Chapter 4 details an evaluation framework for programming implementation and impact customizable to your unique student population, as well as tools to utilize outcomes and feedback to inform and improve practices. When used purposefully, outcomes and feedback can propel an initial idea into a career exploration program that exemplifies best practice.

Additional Best Practices and Lessons Learned

Based on ASA's extensive research, a series of common themes have emerged around best practices and lessons learned:

- It is equally valuable for students to rule an interest or career field "in" as it is for them to determine it is "out." While many of our school partners hope and expect that their programming will inspire new interests, students may also come to realize that something they previously thought they enjoyed may not be for them. This is a valuable lesson to experience during the middle grades while there is still time before major educational and career decisions must be made.
- Students benefit from access to supplemental and ongoing resources to continue career exploration on their own time. These include apps, interest assessments, websites, and other digital tools to complement and enhance their curricular learning.
- Schools were successful when focusing on soft skills and the "building blocks" of careers rather than specific occupations. Students reacted positively to prototyping, goal setting, learning how to navigate failure, collaborative

learning, social-emotional learning, and feeling connected to the "real world." These sorts of flexible and project-based learning opportunities that offered insight into the world of work were, overall, more meaningful to students than restrictive discussions around "what do you want to be when you grow up?"

As planning and programming continues, three key priority areas emerged around next steps:

1. The first is nurturing implementation consistency and working toward broader buy-in across the school community. This includes continued efforts to address the assumption that middle school is too early to begin career discussions.
2. Second is distinguishing career *exploration* from career *decision-making*, including tailoring program language so students do not feel "forced" to decide on any one career path at this point. The goal here is to encourage students to actively discover options so they can learn what appeals to them, what does not, and why.
3. Finally, schools are focused on how to engage families and the broader community, especially in a post-COVID world. As the programs we've studied continue through the grant period and beyond, we are eager to support districts' efforts to leverage community and family resources in the career exploration process.
4. Your program planning and implementation will go far when grounded in these foundational best practices.

NOTES

[1] Advance CTE. (2016). Measuring Work-based Learning for Continuous Improvement. Retrieved on March 15, 2021 from https://cte.careertech.org/sites/default/files/files/resources/WBL_casestudy_measuring_FINAL.pdf

[2] Condliffe, B, et al. (2017). Project-Based Learning: A Literature Review. New York, NY: MDRC.

[3] American Student Assistance. (2018). Survey of 2,393 middle and high school students in the United States, December 2018.

[4] Keiler, L. S. (2018). Teachers' roles and identities in student-centered classrooms. International Journal of STEM Education, 5(1). doi:10.1186/s40594-018-0131-6

[5] Association for Career and Technical Education (ACTE). (2017). Career exploration in middle school: Setting students on the path to success. Alexandria, VA: ACTE and Career Cruising. Retrieved on March 12, 2021 from https://www.acteonline.org/wp-content/uploads/2018/02/ACTE_CC_Paper_FINAL.pdf

[6] Kaput, K. (2018). Evidence for Student-Centered Learning. Saint Paul, Minnesota: Education Evolving. Retrieved on March 15, 2021 from https://www.educationevolving.org/files/Evidence-for-Student-Centered-Learning.pdf

[7] Association for Career and Technical Education (ACTE). (2017). Career exploration in middle school: Setting students on the path to success. Alexandria, VA: ACTE and Career Cruising. Retrieved on March 12, 2021 from https://www.acteonline.org/wp-content/uploads/2018/02/ACTE_CC_Paper_FINAL.pdf

[8] Association for Career and Technical Education (ACTE). (2017). Career exploration in middle school: Setting students on the path to success. Alexandria, VA: ACTE and Career Cruising. Retrieved on March 12, 2021 from https://www.acteonline.org/wp-content/uploads/2018/02/ACTE_CC_Paper_FINAL.pdf

[9] Balfanz, R. (2009). Putting Middle Grades Students on the Graduation Path: A Policy and Practice Brief. Baltimore, MD: Everyone Graduates Center at Johns Hopkins University, Philadelphia Education Fund, and National Middle School Association. Retrieved on March 12, 2021 from https://www.amle.org/portals/0/pdf/articles/policy_brief_balfanz.pdf

[10] Balfanz, R. (2009). Putting Middle Grades Students on the Graduation Path: A Policy and Practice Brief. Baltimore, MD: Everyone Graduates Center at Johns Hopkins University, Philadelphia Education Fund, and National Middle School Association. Retrieved on March 12, 2021 from https://www.amle.org/portals/0/pdf/articles/policy_brief_balfanz.pdf

[11] Rosen, R., & Molina. F. (2019). Practitioner Perspectives on Equity in Career and Technical Education. MDRC Center for Effective Career and Technical Education. Retrieved on March 15, 2021 from https://www.mdrc.org/sites/default/files/CTE_Equity_Brief_2019.pdf

[12] Coalition For Career Development. (2019). Career Readiness For All. Retrieved on March 12, 2021 from https://www.ncda.org/aws/NCDA/asset_manager/get_file/308195?ver=2958

[13] Rosen, R., & Molina. F. (2019). Practitioner Perspectives on Equity in Career and Technical Education. MDRC Center for Effective Career and Technical Education. Retrieved on March 15, 2021 from https://www.mdrc.org/sites/default/files/CTE_Equity_Brief_2019.pdf

[14] Ball, A., Joyce, H. D., & Anderson-Butcher, D. (2016). Exploring 21st century skills and learning environments for middle school youth. *International Journal of School Social Work, 1*(1). doi:10.4148/2161-4148.1012

[15] Association for Career and Technical Education (ACTE). (2017). Career exploration in middle school: Setting students on the path to success. Alexandria, VA: ACTE and Career Cruising. Retrieved on March 12, 2021 from https://www.acteonline.org/wp-content/uploads/2018/02/ACTE_CC_Paper_FINAL.pdf

[16] Ball, A., Joyce, H. D., & Anderson-Butcher, D. (2016). Exploring 21st century skills and learning environments for middle school youth. *International Journal of School Social Work, 1*(1). doi:10.4148/2161-4148.1012

[17] Dove, M., & Freeley, M. E.. (2011). The Effects of Leadership on Effective Program Implementation. Austin, TX. *Delta Kappa Gamma Bulletin.* Vol. 77 Iss.3., 25–33

Chapter 3

Program Planning and Implementation

Career exploration programs can begin at any level in education. This implementation guide and accompanying action plans are designed to support district and school leaders, counselors, and teachers and can be utilized to create any type of career exploration program: whole-school, counselor-centered, STEM or STEAM, work-based learning, project-based learning, or any other innovative model.

For each educator role, programmatic planning begins with the same two steps: 1) establishing a team; and 2) setting clear, measurable goals. A strong, collaborative team is crucial to developing a purposeful career exploration program while increasing buy-in. Establishing clear goals that are achievable and measurable not only focuses the first-year implementation, but also drives planning for future years. Program sustainability should also be prioritized throughout the planning process. Many programs have launched at the beginning of a school year, only to dwindle by summer. A successful, impactful program is designed to endure, as well as to adapt over time to remain relevant and accessible for students.

PROGRAM IMPLEMENTATION GUIDE

Step 1: Establish a Team

The first step toward implementation is to organize a team responsible for planning and implementation. The most successful teams involve all stakeholders from the beginning of planning. Bringing in different perspectives builds buy-in, helps proactively identify and overcome challenges, and creates an effective, relevant, and inclusive program. Ensuring that teachers who will be doing the daily work are included in all steps of the planning process is essential to sustaining a middle school career exploration program.

> **A successful, impactful program is designed to endure, as well as to adapt over time to remain relevant and accessible for students.**

Step 2: Set Clear Measurable Goals

Clear goals drive programmatic decisions, short- and long-term plans, and the overall budget. SMART goals—goals that are **Specific, Measurable, Attainable, Relevant, and Timely**—should be agreed upon by the planning team. The implementation checklists included in chapter 4 are a great starting point to help accomplish this. Aligning programmatic goals with classroom standards and objectives ensures career exploration remains a priority. When developing goals, consider:

- What are the problems/opportunities that need to be addressed by this program?
- How will they be addressed?

Roles for Creating a Team

District/School Leaders	Counselors	Teachers
• Determine who will participate in planning and implementation of the program	• Include district/school leaders throughout the planning process to ensure buy-in	• Include district/school leaders throughout the planning process to ensure buy-in
• Establish a set planning time for initial implementation, as well as check-in opportunities throughout the year	• Collaborate with educators who will be involved in implementation	• Collaborate with educators who will be involved in implementation; utilize the guidance counselors in the building as a resource or colleague to plan with
• Inform additional stakeholders who are essential for program success (grant managers, district leaders, etc.)	• Establish a set planning time for initial implementation, as well as check-in opportunities throughout the year	• Establish a set planning time for initial implementation, as well as additional planning throughout the year
• Include the team in all parts of the process, including setting programmatic goals	• Consider ways to expand programming; connect with teachers to bring career exploration into their classrooms or share work with other guidance counselors in the building or district	• Consider ways to expand programming; collaborate with teachers in different grades or content areas

- What does success look like during the first year of programming, for students, educators, and the school/district?
- How will progress be measured?

- How will programming expand over the next few years?

Roles for Setting Goals

District/School Leaders	Counselors	Teachers
• Establish attainable goals for the school year that could be expanded and adapted over the next few years • Break down district, school, and classroom-specific goals • Analyze current data to notice gaps and trends • Create a data plan to measure progress • Align goals to state or national standards	• Establish attainable goals for the school year that could be expanded and adapted over the next few years • Utilize backwards planning while determining programmatic goals • Analyze current data to notice gaps and trends • Create a data plan to measure progress • Align goals to state or national standards and classroom objectives	• Establish attainable goals for the school year that could be expanded and adapted over the next few years • Utilize backwards planning while determining programmatic goals • Analyze current data to notice gaps and trends • Create a data plan to measure progress • Align goals to state or national standards and classroom objectives

Step 3: Develop a Program Plan

In this step, the planning team determines program specifics, including which model to adopt, which grade levels and content areas will be included, whether the program will be a pilot or whole-school rollout, and how programming will be implemented. The team evaluates various supplementary programs and products to determine what to purchase, or if to instead create their own. The team should use data to drive decisions and be selective about which programs or products to use. Taking on too many resources at once can be overwhelming and difficult to execute.

Whole-school buy-in should be prioritized throughout the project plan and should include ways to promote programming, share successes, and provide opportunities for stakeholders to observe and learn. Professional development is crucial to program sustainability and should be mapped out for the initial year as well as extended over the following years.

Creating a budget is also an important part of step 3. The planning team should consider what resources are needed, and where funds will come from, including if district funds are available to support the program or if grants from outside organizations will be needed.

Step 4: Develop Plans for Family Engagement, Community Engagement, and Program Sustainability

A successful, long-lasting career exploration plan considers family engagement, strong relationships with community partners, and program sustainability. These steps generally don't vary by role, so this is a more generalized list of action items.

Family Engagement

We know that family engagement contributes to positive academic and career outcomes for students.[1] Every family engagement plan is different and considers the district's unique community. When a school/district creates opportunities for families to learn about, support, and engage with their middle schoolers' career exploration, students can build connections beyond the classroom walls.

Create a communication plan to keep families informed of the program and of opportunities for their children; provide translations so all families can engage.

Career Exploration in the Middle Grades

District/School Leaders	Counselors	Teachers
Together, the team should: • **Determine how programming will be implemented; and** • **Decide on programming specifics.**			
In their individual roles, educators will:			
• Evaluate programs or products, or determine whether the school district will create their own curriculum • Develop a plan for lesson and program observations • Build in Professional Development (PD) throughout the year; determine who will receive trainings and how PD will continue during the next few years of programming • Create a budget and determine where that funding could come from • Build methods to increase educator buy-in throughout the plan • Map out events, field trips, and project showcases throughout the year	• Build programming plans for larger groups of students, as well as pull-out groups or one-on-one activities • Evaluate programs or products, or determine whether to create a curriculum • Create a budget, and share with school or district leaders to determine funding • Map out events, field trips, and project showcases throughout the year • Look for Professional Development opportunities	• Develop a plan throughout the school year by mapping out full units of content or when specific lessons or projects will occur • Evaluate programs or products, or determine whether to create a curriculum • Gather instructional resources • Consider building a makerspace in the classroom • Create a budget, and share with school or district leaders to determine funding • Map out what events will occur, and when • Look for Professional Development opportunities

Organize virtual and in-person informational sessions families can attend to learn about the program, ask questions, and hear how they can be involved/supportive.

- Create family resources with information about the program and steps they can take to support their child as they engage in career exploration projects and skill-building activities.
- Develop sessions for families to participate in career exploration themselves and create opportunities for them to take advantage of the program to gain career-related opportunities.
- Connect with family members who work in the community and can participate in programming as a professional or business partner.
- Plan summative events, like project showcases or student-led conferences for families to see student work in action.

CASE STUDY: Using Family and Community Engagement to Drive Program Success

STEM Middle Academy, Springfield, Massachusetts

STEM Middle Academy is a diverse grade 6–8 school located in a low socioeconomic area. Our career exploration program has greatly improved student engagement and interest in a variety of careers, and increased students' access to phenomenon-driven activities in science and technology. We also have science inclusion programs for students with disabilities and special needs, allowing our program to reach almost our entire student population. Planning and implementation is a collaboration between the science department, administration, and teachers willing to support cross-curricular events.

Prior to this program, career exploration was done in a reading and research manner with few opportunities for students to experience these fields. Our new career exploration initiative began with a professionality-centered program to support career skills in all types of trades, fields, and occupations. Since its inception, we have evolved greatly. Our focus has moved to encouraging all students, especially girls and students of color, to explore career fields that they may not have considered. We have been able to spark important discussions on the kinds of barriers students may face in entering fields that traditionally lack diversity.

Importantly, family and community engagement continues to increase with each new phase of this program. Parents are engaged as they see projects and prototypes being brought home. As they explore, students are especially attracted to professional roles held by students' friends and family members, thereby establishing a sense of community relevance to career opportunities within the city. Families are able to assist in an 8th grade career research project because many students chose careers with which their families are familiar. Parent engagement became more difficult due to COVID and remote learning. We pivoted to virtual field trips to allow students to meet experts and engage with community members from home:

- Eighth grade students spent time with the VP of Visual Effects at Marvel Studios, and members of her VFX design team. She took them on a virtual field trip, answered student questions about her career path, and connected student interests in science, art, and video

games to career paths in computer programming, VFX architecture, and design.
- Seventh grade students met with our local city planning department. Our speaker described her job as a city planner and the educational journey she had to complete to reach the position she holds today. Students were inspired to know that there is more than one path they can follow to find a role that makes a difference in their local community.
- Sixth grade students took a virtual field trip with NASA. The speaker explained life as a lunar scientist, which connected to the classroom where students were simultaneously learning about the phases of the moon.

To reach our current level of family engagement took a great deal of tenacity and a variety of communication methods that included:

- Calling families
- Posting notifications and messages on our school platform
- Mailing letter to families
- Social media advertisements

Because of these efforts, we see family and community engagement only increasing as the program continues.

Luis Martinez, Principal, Katherine Carman, 7th grade Science Teacher, and Chris McCarthy, 8th grade Department Head and Science Teacher

Community Engagement

The school/district should seek community partners who are interested in supporting and participating in the program. Strong relationships with community partners take time to develop; start with current personal and professional connections and build from there. Community partner involvement can create real-world connections for students while extending programming to include experiential opportunities. It may be tempting to table this process and focus on other components, but these relationships are essential to creating a dynamic career exploration program. Designate a planning team member or sub-team to focus on developing and fostering community partnerships.

- Create a network of community partners by utilizing professional and personal connections; maintain a list of partners and build from there.
- Send letters to local businesses and organizations to engage them in partnership work.
- Partner with local businesses to establish work-based opportunities for students.
- Design events where community partners can be involved, such as: project showcases, contest/challenge judging panels, career days, classroom interviews, and community spotlights.
- Utilize digital tools to connect with geographically diverse professionals, allowing you to engage partners around the world.
- Establish a mentorship program to connect students to local professionals.
- Create project- and design-based challenges connected to the local community.

CASE STUDY: Leveraging Community Connections Through a Unified Approach

KIPP Massachusetts, Boston and Lynn, Massachusetts

KIPP Massachusetts encompasses five schools across two districts in Boston and Lynn and has been educating students for over 15 years. Our mission is that together, with families and communities, we create joyful, academically excellent schools that prepare students with the skills and confidence to pursue the paths they choose—college, career, and beyond—so they can lead fulfilling lives and build a more just world. Part of fulfilling our mission means providing impactful career learning experiences. We have been using the Project Lead The Way (PLTW) curriculum over the past four years, which provides rich STEM learning experiences for our middle school students.

While this programming has been impactful, we knew we could take it further by using it to connect students to related STEM careers. High school Science Teacher Allen Wang said it best: "You can't be what you can't see." Through conversations with curriculum specialists, science teachers, and middle and high school leaders, we developed a plan to expose our middle school students to more meaningful career connections.

Career fairs and industry talks are helpful, but they sometimes fail to create an authentic connection between students and careers. We felt that our PLTW projects provided an excellent opportunity to foster these connections. We began inviting engineers, programmers, designers, and doctors to provide feedback to our students on their projects.

We found that it can be overwhelming for teachers to have to manage the connections and coordination with outside partners, so we try to take care of that at the regional level. For context, we have two regional team members dedicated to our science and STEM curriculum and teacher support across our five schools. One team member supports our K–4th grade teachers and students, and one team member supports 5th–12th grade teachers and students. These regional team members support the external side of making career connections. After our team members find volunteers through inquiries to local industry, they also maintain an unofficial database of individuals who have participated. We find that many of these volunteers love to come back again and again. It also helps to have teachers communicate to the volunteers beforehand (via email, phone call, or even a pre-recorded video) to explain the project and student expectations. Volunteers feel more prepared to engage meaningfully with students.

We have found that these interactions with industry professionals are more impactful, because rather than simply "hearing about" a career, students get to work with an industry expert directly on an actual project. We have set the ambitious goal that every year, every single student in our middle schools will present a STEM project to an industry expert. Students have already found these interactions valuable. "I always assumed an engineer is someone who works on cars!" said one 8th grade student after working with a General Electric (GE) engineer on a design project. Our students continue to show enthusiasm for project-based learning that leads to feedback and conversations with industry professionals. We are excited to continue this program and look forward to deepening our partnerships once students return to the building next school year!

Jay Galbraith, Director of Secondary Science, and Rebecca Hazlett, Development and External Relations Manager

Sustainability and Grant Funding

A program that fizzles out after one year will not produce the same positive outcomes as one that is purposely built to sustain and grow. Building a community of practice by leveraging family and community engagement can improve your odds of creating an impactful, sustainable middle grades career exploration program.

- Develop three-year and five-year programmatic plans, and revisit these plans throughout the year to continue to adjust and set goals.
- Create a budget and identify additional sources of funding.
- Focus on scale. Can the program extend beyond the initial classroom, grade level, or school?
- Create a plan for stakeholder buy-in.
- Maintain practices and routines that build this program into the school's culture.
- Create long-term professional development plans that build educator knowledge while also training new staff.

Visit the Resource Center for a listing of current funding opportunities and a library of resources, including tips for writing a successful grant proposal.

Career Exploration Implementation Action Guides

The following Career Exploration Implementation Action Guides provide a helpful checklist and guiding questions/tips to aid in your planning process. Visit the Resource Center for the latest, downloadable versions.

CAREER EXPLORATION IN THE MIDDLE GRADES

District/School Leader
Career Exploration Action Guide - Part 1

Step 1: Establish a Team

Documents/To-Do Items	Guiding Questions & Tips
☐ Finalize list of team members ☐ Establish initial planning session ☐ Create a schedule of team check-ins ☐ Develop team norms and best practices ☐ Notify additional stakeholders of the program (ex: grant managers, researchers, district leaders, etc.). This may include creating an outreach plan.	Who will be involved in program planning? Include: • Teachers • Counselors • Educational Leaders • District Members Does the initial planning session provide enough time for collaboration? Will multiple sessions be needed? Be strategic with check-ins. Consider who should attend each check-in and how often the team meets. Ex: school personnel implementing the program in their classrooms may need consistent check-ins while the entire group may meet on a different schedule. Visit or virtually connect with other schools with career exploration programs to observe and ask questions.

Step 2: Set Clear, Measurable Goals

Documents/To-Do Items	Guiding Questions & Tips
☐ Write a short program overview ☐ Create year one goals ☐ Align goals with applicable standards ☐ Create post-implementation long-term goals ☐ Review and analyze current data ☐ Develop an initial program measurement and assessment strategy	Questions to ask while planning: • What are the problems that need to be addressed by this program? • How will they be addressed? • What does success look like during the program's first year, for students, educators, and the school/district? • How will progress be measured? Break down goals by district, school, and classroom: • Do all of these goals align with one another? • How can goals be used to increase collaboration among team members? • What are some goals for students? When analyzing data, ask: • Where are there gaps in current programming? • What opportunities exist? • What is missing from current data collection methods? Reference Chapter 4 for program measurement and assessment recommendations and resources.

Program Planning and Implementation

District/School Leader
Career Exploration Action Guide - Part 2

Step 3: Develop a Program Plan

Documents/To-Do Items	Guiding Questions & Tips
☐ Develop a specific program plan ☐ Build in strategies to increase educator buy-in throughout implementation ☐ Determine a strategy to evaluate supportive programs and products and begin evaluation ☐ Develop an observation plan and schedule ☐ Develop a profressional development plan and map out sessions throughout the year ☐ Create the program budget ☐ Make a list of funding opportunities ☐ Schedule program events, like project showcases and field trips	Questions to ask while planning: • What kind of program do you want to create? • How will the program be implemented? • Who will be able to access the program? Consider ways to include other educators in the work and how to share best practices as they emerge. Be purposeful about which products and programs to adopt. Taking on too many at once can be overwhelming. Consider starting as a pilot, by beginning in one classroom, grade level, or school in the district. Plan PD purposefully: think about how trainings can build on each other over the next few years, as well as how new staff will be trained.

Step 4: Family and Community Engagement

Documents/To-Do Items	Guiding Questions & Tips
Part a: Family Engagement ☐ Develop a family communication plan ☐ Plan information sessions ☐ Build a library of resources for families to learn about and engage with the program ☐ Include families in program event planning **Part b: Community Engagement** ☐ Create a list of personal/professional connections within the community ☐ Create a community outreach plan ☐ Map how to engage partners in the planning ☐ Include community in progam event plans ☐ Evaluate tools and platforms that utilize industry connections ☐ Create a plan for a mentorship program	Provide translations of all communications and include students in family events. Encourage students to share projects at student-led conferences. Consider creating opportunities for families to learn about career exploration themselves, and to take advantage of the program. Equip families with lists of external opportuntiies for students to explore their interests. Consider having a point person that will prioritize engaging community partners. They should seek partners from diverse backgrounds and fields. Build projects around communities issues to make real-world connections for students. Ways to engage partners include: • Mentorships • Work-based learning opportunities • Project showcases • Contests • Career Days • Professional interviews • Community spotlights

CAREER EXPLORATION IN THE MIDDLE GRADES

School Counselor
Career Exploration Action Guide - Part 1

Step 1: Establish a Team

Documents/To-Do Items	Guiding Questions & Tips
☐ Set up conversations with district/school leaders to engage them throughout the planning and implementation process ☐ Make a list of educators to collaborate with ☐ Establish a set planning time for initial implementation, as well as check-in opportunities throughout the year ☐ Consider ways to expand programming throughout the year.	Starting with conversations with leadership is crucial for garnering support, and possible funding, for a program. Reach out to different educators to see if there is interest. Think about including colleagues with varied backgrounds and experience in the planning process. Connect with other counselors in the school/district. • Observe other school's programs • Collaborate on ideas and resources Does the initial planning session provide enough time for collaboration? Should you plan multiple sessions? Be purposeful with meeting planning. From the start, set team norms and best practices.

Step 2: Set Clear, Measurable Goals

Documents/To-Do Items	Guiding Questions & Tips
☐ Write a short program overview ☐ Create year one goals ☐ Align goals with applicable standards ☐ Create long-term goals ☐ Review and analyze current data ☐ Develop an initial program measurement and assessment strategy	Questions to ask while planning: • What are the problems that need to be addressed by this program? • How will they be addressed? • What does success look like during the program's first year, for students, educators, and the school/district? • How will progress be measured? • How can goals be used to increase collaboration among team members? When analyzing data, ask: • Where are there gaps in current programming? • What opportunities exist? • What is missing from current data collection methods? Reference Chapter 4 for program measurement and assessment recommendations and resources.

Program Planning and Implementation

School Counselor
Career Exploration Action Guide - Part 2

Step 3: Develop a Program Plan

Documents/To-Do Items	Guiding Questions & Tips
☐ Develop a specific program plan ☐ Evaluate programs or products, or determine whether to create your own curriculum ☐ Create a program budget, and share with district/school leaders to determine a funding strategy ☐ Seek external funding opportunities ☐ Develop a profressional development plan and map out sessions throughout the year ☐ Schedule program events, like project showcases and field trips	Questions to ask while planning: • What kind of program do you want to create? • How will the program be implemented? • Who will be able to access the program? Be purposeful about which products and programs to adopt. Taking on too many at once can be overwhelming. Backwards plan while deciding what activities, such as project showcases, field trips, and student activities, to include to develop a more robust program. Build programming plans for larger groups of studenets, as well as pull-out groups or one-on-ones. Consider ways to engage district/school leaders and colleagues in events.

Step 4: Family and Community Engagement

Documents/To-Do Items	Guiding Questions & Tips
Part a: Family Engagement ☐ Develop a family communication plan ☐ Plan information sessions ☐ Build a library of resources for families to learn about and engage with the program ☐ Include families in program event planning **Part b: Community Engagement** ☐ Create a list of personal/professional connections within the community ☐ Create a community outreach plan ☐ Map how to engage partners in the planning ☐ Include community in progam event plans ☐ Evaluate tools and platforms that utilize industry connections ☐ Create a plan for a mentorship program	Provide translations of all communications and include students in family events. Encourage students to share projects at student-led conferences. Consider creating opportunities for families to learn about career exploration themselves, and to take advantage of the program. Equip families with lists of external opportunties for students to explore their interests. Consider having a point person that will prioritize engaging community partners. They should seek partners from diverse backgrounds and fields. Build projects around communities issues to make real-world connections for students. Ways to engage partners include: • Mentorships • Work-based learning opportunities • Project showcases • Contests • Career Days • Professional interviews • Community spotlights

CAREER EXPLORATION IN THE MIDDLE GRADES

Teacher
Career Exploration Action Guide - Part 1

Step 1: Establish a Team

Documents/To-Do Items	Guiding Questions & Tips
☐ Set up conversations with district/school leaders to engage them throughout the planning and implementation process ☐ Make a list of colleagues to collaborate with ☐ Establish a set planning time for initial implementation, as well as check-in opportunities throughout the year ☐ Consider ways to expand programming throughout the year	Starting with conversations with leadership is crucial for garnering support, and possible funding, for a program. Reach out to different colleagues to see if there is interest, and think about creating a diverse team with varyied experiences: • Consider collaborating across grade levels or content areas for a more holistic approach. • Use counselors as a resource. Ask what programming has already occured, what resources are available, and opportunities to collaborate. Does the initial planning session provide enough time for collaboration? Should you plan multiple sessions? Be purposeful with meeting planning. From the start, set team norms and best practices.

Step 2: Set Clear, Measurable Goals

Documents/To-Do Items	Guiding Questions & Tips
☐ Write a short program overview ☐ Create year one goals ☐ Align goals with applicable standards ☐ Create long-term goals ☐ Review and analyze current data ☐ Develop an initial program measurement and assessment strategy	Questions to ask while planning: • What are the problems that need to be addressed by this program? • How will they be addressed? • What does success look like during the program's first year, for students, educators, and the school/district? • How will progress be measured? • How can goals be used to increase collaboration among team members? • What are goals for students? When analyzing classroom data, ask: • Where are there gaps in current programming? • What opportunities exist? • What is missing from current data collection methods? Reference Chapter 4 for program measurement and assessment recommendations and resources.

Program Planning and Implementation

Teacher
Career Exploration Action Guide - Part 2

Step 3: Develop a Program Plan

Documents/To-Do Items	Guiding Questions & Tips
☐ Develop a specific program plan ☐ Plan units and lessons for the semester ☐ Evaluate programs or products, or determine whether to create your own curriculum ☐ Gather instructional resources. ☐ Create a budget, share with district/school leaders to determine a funding strategy ☐ Seek external funding opportunities ☐ Plan proffessional development plan and map out sessions throughout the year ☐ Schedule program events, like project showcases and field trips	Questions to ask while planning: • What kind of program do you want to create? • How will the program be implemented? • Who will be able to access the program? Be purposeful about which products and programs to adopt. Taking on too many at once can be overwhelming. Backwards plan units, especially while making decisions about project showcases, field trips, and student activites to develop a more comprehensive program/curriculum. Consider building a makerspace in your classroom that students can utilize throughout the year. Consider ways to engage district/school leaders and colleagues in events.

Step 4: Family and Community Engagement

Documents/To-Do Items	Guiding Questions & Tips
Part a: Family Engagement ☐ Develop a family communication plan ☐ Plan information sessions ☐ Build a library of resources for families to learn about and engage with the program ☐ Include families in program event planning **Part b: Community Engagement** ☐ Create a list of personal/professional connections within the community ☐ Create a community outreach plan ☐ Map how to engage partners in the planning ☐ Include community in progam event plans ☐ Evaluate tools and platforms that utilize industry connections ☐ Create a plan for a mentorship program	Provide translations of all communications and include students in family events. Encourage students to share projects at student-led conferences. Consider creating opportunities for families to learn about career exploration themselves, and to take advantage of the program. Equip families with lists of external opportuntiies for students to explore their interests. Consider having a point person that will prioritize engaging community partners. They should seek partners from diverse backgrounds and fields. Build projects around communities issues to make real-world connections for students. Ways to engage partners include: • Mentorships • Work-based learning opportunities • Project showcases • Contests • Career Days • Professional interviews • Community spotlights

All Roles - Program Sustainability
Career Exploration Action Guide

Documents/To-Do Items	Guiding Questions & Tips
☐ Develop a 3-year and 5-year plan ☐ Create a long-term budget ☐ Make a running list of additional funding sources and opportunities, including grants ☐ Create a plan for stakeholder buy-in ☐ Create a plan for scaling programming ☐ Develop a long-term professional development plan	As you plan for sustainability, ask these questions: • What does long-term program success look like? • How can this program continue to grow? • What long-term funding opportunities are available? • Who will continue to champion the program and how will they maintain it? • What are some long-term goals in regards to the impact on students?

NOTES

[1]Henderson, A.T. & Berla, Nancy (1994). A New Generation of Evidence: The Family is Critical to Student Achievement. Washington, DC: National Committee for Students in Education. Retrieved on March 25, 2021 from https://files.eric.ed.gov/fulltext/ED375968.pdf

Chapter 4

Program Assessment and Measurement

In any student-facing programming, the most important questions are often the simplest: **Why** are we providing this opportunity to students and **what** do we hope to see as a result? Starting with these questions helps establish clear program goals, ensure intentionality in the program's design, and cultivate at least a general understanding of what a successful program might look like. As we regularly check in on what students are enjoying, what is most engaging, and what types of events or tools are most interesting or useful, the feedback we collect can be used formatively to drive continuous improvement in programming at the school and classroom level.

Program evaluations are systematic approaches for measuring program effectiveness, learning what works, and highlighting potential areas for improvement. They can help answer questions such as:

- Is our program working as intended?
- Is our program serving all students equitably?
- Are educators and staff aware of our goals?
- What are the barriers to meeting our goals, and how can we overcome them?

By leveraging various research frameworks and data sources, a quality evaluation approach ensures that program implementation and program impact are measured with special attention to local considerations while also maintaining a high degree of rigor. This chapter outlines our approach, offering a how-to guide as you seek to measure program efficacy in your own school/district.

Implementation v. Impact

First, we should distinguish between **implementation** and **impact**. Program implementation covers logistics, opportunities, barriers, and the actual set up and running of the program. Impact, conversely, is centered on outcomes and results. Schools/districts seeking to create a program from scratch or pilot an existing program for the first time might consider studying implementation specifically, in addition to impact. Why? If a program is not being implemented as intended, then any outcome measures related to impact may be flawed or incomplete. This is especially important for multi-year or other longitudinal engagements that depend on successful rollout in the first year.

> **As we regularly check in on what students are enjoying, what is most engaging, and what types of events or tools are most interesting or useful, the feedback we collect can be used formatively to drive continuous improvement in programming at the school and classroom level.**

We recommend using process evaluation techniques to study implementation, and outcome evaluation techniques to study impact. This table presents typical questions that might be addressed in a process evaluation versus an outcome evaluation.

Program Assessment and Measurement

PROCESS EVALUATION (Implementation)	OUTCOME EVALUATION (Impact)
• How is program rollout going? • Is the program being rolled out as intended? • Are students aware of and able to access all components of the program? • To what extent are school staff aware of and interested in the program?	• Have students reacted positively to the program and its components? • As a result of the program, are students changing in their attitudes and beliefs? • Are students improving in the target outcomes the program is designed to address? • What are the short-term and long-term effects of the program?

CASE STUDY: Leveraging Program Data, and a Student-Centered Approach to Drive Program Success

Taunton Public Schools, Taunton, Massachusetts

The Taunton Public Schools STEM and Career Exploration program for middle school learners is in its second year at Friedman and Martin Middle Schools and we will begin implementation at our third school, Parker Middle, next fall. Each student takes the STEM class as part of the arts rotation at each school and the curriculum is based on Project Lead the Way's Gateway curriculum (Computer Science for Innovators & Makers, and Design & Modeling). This is a new program that was developed to meet our district's goal of enriching STEM learning experiences for middle school students with the hopes of increasing the number of students who pursue STEM education and careers as part of their postsecondary pursuits.

Initially, the planning team included district curriculum leaders and school leadership. Now, the wind in our sails comes from student voices. As the Science Curriculum Coordinator, I work closely with the teachers at these schools, examining data from student surveys, classroom observations, and grade level meetings to understand what aspects of this curriculum meet students' motivational needs and can create bridges between the STEM class and other subjects. The intent of these connections is twofold. First, they show students that STEM impacts their daily lives. Second, it gives all educators license to speak about how their disciplines factor into students' future careers in limitless ways. We found that fluidity is important. Nothing in middle school should exist in a bubble; being responsive to students' changing educational landscape and their evolving needs has helped us nurture a motivating learning community. This type of class is fertile ground for relationship building and, therefore, teachers are able to have goal setting discussions with students and plan opportunities for students to learn about careers in a differentiated fashion. We currently measure our success through student surveys and with traditional measures like grades and engagement. Soon we will be tracking students as they enter high school and seeing if they enter into one of the career pathways outlined at the high school.

A difficulty we face is curbing the impulse to grow this program by adding more STEM initiatives to this class. While an understandable goal, being protective of the class structure has given the teachers the space and autonomy to continue focusing on career exploration. This class now prepares students for career pathways at the high school level because they have a stronger sense of what they want to and do not want to explore. We have also had a difficult time planning career exploration opportunity with students because, due to the nature of remote learning, students are hesitant to attend events outside of school time. We hope that when we return to normalcy, we can reach out to families, local universities, and our industry partners to talk to our students and, hopefully, provide mentoring opportunities. We believe that students must talk about their futures early and often in order to truly believe that they are capable of reaching any career or educational goal.

My advice for other schools embarking on this journey would be to put students first. There will be people who want to add to your program in one way or another, and you may feel this takes your program in a different direction. If you stay focused on students' motivational needs, your program will be a success.

Elizabeth Pawlowski, Science Curriculum Coordinator

Approaching Program Evaluation

We recommend a concurrent mixed-methods approach, drawing from a variety of data sources to measure what is working well and what might need some attention. Essentially, this involves collecting both quantitative data (e.g., student surveys, demographic data, and other types of quantifiable measures) and qualitative data (e.g., open-ended feedback, classroom observations, and other types of descriptive data). Educators can leverage *quantitative* data collection to study trends across programs and student subgroups, and *qualitative* data to richly understand the student experience, classroom engagement, and program implementation.

In ASA's own work, data sources are collected throughout the academic year and include surveys for both students and educators, demographic data, course data, classroom observations, and opportunities for educator feedback during regular "check-in" sessions.

Stakeholder engagement is also key. You may consider developing a year-end impact report that can be shared. This report might include a one-page summary of major highlights, student demographics, changes in student attitudes from the beginning to the end of the year, reactions at the end of the year, and major likes and dislikes associated with the programming. Below is a selection from a report prepared by ASA to provide you with some direction in creating your own:

SATISFACTION	Students who participated in career exploration programming at our partner schools were 39 percent more satisfied with the school year than their peers who did not participate.
FUTURE PLANNING	Compared to students not participating in the career exploration programming, participating students were significantly more likely to have a clear plan for their life after high school, more likely to report that their school provided them the opportunity to explore their unique skills and interests, and less nervous about their future overall. In the second full year of programming, we also noted significantly higher confidence among participating students around knowing their options and navigating future educational and career planning.
HIGH SCHOOL COURSEWORK	Throughout the school year, students made significant gains in their high school planning. One in three students who were not thinking about taking career-related courses in high school became interested by the end of the year, and one in four students who were not thinking about classes to help them prepare for college reported interest by the end of the year. Said one student, **"I like that it talked about how to be able to figure out what you want to do, and you can take classes next year about it."**

CLASSROOM ENGAGEMENT	During classroom observations, both in-person (pre-COVID) and virtual, we noted high participation and engagement among students, especially during group work, project-based learning activities, and career days.
STUDENT FEEDBACK	"This year's opportunities gave me a chance to discover more about what I like and dislike in the career fields, and it helped me decide what I want to do in high school especially because I have more of a choice next year about what I want to do." – *Mary, grade 7* "Something I liked about the career exploration opportunities was that it showed me what I was interested in and what traits I have to help me with a specific job." – *Duane, grade 6* "I liked how we got to think about others and create something that other people could use in life to help with their disabilities." – *Ava, grade 7*

Program Assessment and Evaluation: A How-To Guide

Our evaluation strategy might look different from your own due to staffing, capacity, timing, or a variety of other factors. Evaluation can take many different forms while remaining useful and informative. Recognizing that many educators may not have access to external researchers, the Middle School Programming Outcomes Worksheet offers an accessible, step-by-step guide to establishing an intentional and actionable measurement approach in your own settings. These worksheets are not meant to replace a professional researcher, which you may find helpful to engage in your work, but rather make it more accessible and useful in your classroom or school settings. Visit the Resource Center for downloadable versions of the worksheet and sample program reports and templates.

Career Exploration Programming Outcomes Worksheet - Part 1

Step 1 - Planning: By completing this worksheet, you will make progress toward ensuring goals are intentional and any outcomes that you measure are directly tied to the program.

Brainstorming	Notes
WHY are we providing this opportunity to students? • Clarify the goal(s) of the program • Specify how the program might be essentially useful or impactful in your school, district, or community • Share what "problem" or missing opportunities the program is intended to address **WHAT do we hope to see as a result?** • Ensure programming is intentional/purposeful • Consider the desired changes in students' attitudes, beliefs, academic performance, etc. **HOW are we expecting to improve student outcomes?** • Outline the mechanisms through which programming should, ideally, impact students' attitudes, beliefs, academic performance, andy other outcomes specified above • Remember to be intentional in programming goals	
Logistics	**Notes**
WHO are we aiming to serve? • Identify the student group(s), class(es), or grade level(s) that are the target audience of the program. **WHO are the program champions/stakeholders?** • Identify the educators, leaders, partners, community members, and others who are interested in or would be directly impacted by the program results **WHAT is the timeline?** • Decide when the program will begin and end • Determine at which points outcomes/reporting is needed • Clarify whether there will be multiple cohorts of students entering the program at different times	
Checklist	

- Identify how program data/results will be used
- Determine who will oversee outcomes measurement and reporting
- Review "Brainstorming" questions with key stakeholders to help nurture a culture of shared goals

Program Assessment and Measurement

Career Exploration Programming Outcomes Worksheet - Part 2

Step 2 - Anaylsis: In this section, you will clarify goals and specify exactly what to measure. Completing this chart with key stakeholders will help cultivate a shared understanding of what needs to be measured, why, and how.

Data Sources

Select how you might try to measure the short- and long-term outcomes measured above. If your program is focused on student engagement and attendance, then a school file will contain the attendance records needed. If your program focuses on confidence, then student surveys may be more helpful. "Data" takes many different forms, from school records, to surveys, to student-developed podcast episodes. Be creative and open-minded in how to measure impact!

What are we measuring?	Data Source(s)	Notes
Ex: Students' access to a trusted mentor	Year-end student survey	Ask about WHO the mentor is (parent, coach, etc.) and HOW OFTEN they communicate

Checklist

- Determine whether you can measure effectively with existing data sources, or if a new tool is needed (e.g., a student survey or teacher feedback instrument)
- Consider a wide array of data sources and collection methods, and make intentional choices about what is logical for your setting
- Consider data confidentiality and other ethical concerns, and navigate with care

Step 3 - Review: In this section, you will share results informed by data, discuss implications, and talk through review questions to help summarize the program's impact.

Reporting

Once you have collected and reviewed program data, it is important to analyze results, make informed conclusions, and share findings with interested parties. This does not have to be a formal written report; there are many ways to communicate program effectiveness and recommended next steps. Key elements include program details, a summary of program results, demographic information about the students, select findings, and a summary of recommendations, questions, and next steps. **Visit the online resource center for a library of sample reports and templates.**

Review Questions

These open-ended questions can aid discussions about program planning, implementation, and review (adapted from Mertens and Wilson (2018):
- To what extent were the goals achieved?
- What were/are the major factors influencing achievement/non-achievement of goals?
- Do outcomes vary for different groups of students?
- What happened as a result of the progrma?
- What real difference has the program made to students, staff, or the larger community?

Common Challenges in Program Assessment and Evaluation

Some of the most common challenges in measuring program impact are:

- Setting clear expectations and definitions regarding what to measure;
- Ensuring capacity to measure and report results; and
- Reacting to "bad" results.

Capacity issues vary from school to school, but with the right mindset and guidelines, anyone can develop the ability to clearly define goals, connect them to the program, and specify what needs to be measured as a source of evidence. With that in mind, the guidelines and worksheets in this chapter are meant to encourage and build confidence in your ability to measure program effectiveness in your own settings.

When it comes to collecting feedback or results from a school-based program, there is often a tendency to collect as much data as possible in an effort to "prove" whether something is working. This is often not effective, as the *quantity* of data is inherently prioritized over and above the *quality* of feedback. Instead, our recommended best practice is to start with those early fundamental questions: **Why** are we providing this opportunity to students and **what** do we hope to see as a result? What specific area(s) of growth or learning are desired for students, fellow educators, or the school community at large? This type of thinking clarifies your focus to determine what outcomes to collect. Precise data is more useful than abundant data without a clear focus.

Even with the best intentions, sometimes student programs just do not work well. Despite careful planning, there is always the possibility of finding no growth or growth in the wrong direction on target outcomes. It is also possible that students will not *like* the programming, regardless of outcomes. A strong evaluation system can help catch this early and allow for the opportunity to course-correct. ASA has experienced negative results in our own district work, where despite strong growth on our high school planning and confidence indicators, students sometimes felt pressure to "decide" on their future and sometimes felt like the programming was not inclusive of their personal interests. While not what the school wanted to see, these results provided clarity and a clear path forward to expand what was working and scale back what wasn't. The rich qualitative feedback from students helped identify common pain points while also providing school leaders with ideas for improved inclusion through new offerings. Even "bad" results can be good when leveraged toward program improvement!

Measuring outcomes is doable and critically important for program sustainability. Hopefully, this chapter has made the process approachable for any planning team. An evaluation strategy can entail multi-year, mixed-methods research with advanced analytics conducted by a team of professional researchers. An evaluation strategy can also involve a small group of dedicated educators brainstorming key goals for their students, being intentional about connecting program elements to desired outcomes, and tracking student feedback and academic achievement once a year as they relate specifically to those goals.

Chapter 5

Building a Community of Practice

Thus far we have reviewed the types of career exploration programming, detailed the characteristics of effective programs, provided a framework for implementing a sustainable program, and included resources for evaluating and improving on your program over time. By following this roadmap and utilizing the accompanying online Resource Center, a planning team will be well on their way to a long-lasting, successful program.

There will be challenges along the way. Prioritizing career exploration can be incredibly difficult when there are academic standards and assessments to focus on and student social-emotional needs to address. But it is possible with a strong community of practice. In the preceding chapters, we explored the many stakeholders (students, staff, families, community partners, funders) that need to be engaged to make career exploration programming work. Just as

> **If career exploration for ALL students is a priority for the school community, it will be evident across school activities and in how it is communicated by all school staff—not just leadership.**

career exploration programming must be more than a one-day or one-off event, the culture needed to support an effective program must be more than a slogan.

Culture refers to the interactions among these stakeholders, the words that are spoken, the way we make others feel, and how aligned our behaviors and practices are to the school's values, beliefs, and overall goals. If career exploration for ALL students is a priority for the school community, it will be evident across school activities and in how it is communicated by all school staff—not just leadership.

CASE STUDY: The Launch Pad: A Career Center Reimagined

Cajon Valley Union School District, El Cajon, California

The Cajon Valley Union School District serves a diverse community of 17,000 TK through 12th year students across 28 schools in eastern San Diego County. Since 2017 we have integrated a modern curriculum known as the World of Work™ (WoW), a career development framework grounded in career theory for every child in every grade starting in kindergarten. The unique approach is deployed by teachers who integrate the experiences and a gateway technology in classrooms.

Many teachers have risen to the WoW challenge and built strong communities of practice co-inspired by the district vision of developing happy kids living in healthy relationships on a path to gainful employment. Across the district, the work of helping every child know themselves, know their options, and making informed choices is becoming a reality.

As communities of practice continue to advance within the district, there was one external organization that was considering new ways to share its resources more effectively with K12 schools. The San Diego Workforce Partnership (SDWP) is the "workforce board" for the San Diego County region. As a quasi-governmental entity, they are also a nonprofit, funded through the US Department of Labor. There are 550 workforce boards across the nation that primarily deploy the federal funds to regional partners who then deliver services to adults who are laid off, and need reskilling and support services to regain employment. SDWP has worked to significantly expand the limited impact of a traditional workforce board. By diversifying their funding with many private sector and philanthropic partners, they are reimagining what it means to do workforce development. Among their innovations is to deploy their labor market research with educational tools and technology—reaching and empowering job seekers of all ages with personalized career pathways exploration that is navigable and impactful.

In the spring of 2019, with the support of American Student Assistance, a new community of practice and strategic project was initiated between the Cajon Valley Union School District and the San Diego Workforce Partnership. The goal was to expand the reach of the SDWP tools and data, and leverage the World of Work™ framework to reimagine a middle-school library space and transform it into a WoW-inspired career center. It is called the Launch Pad.

Together with SDWP, we created a community building process for feedback generation to ensure the designs would meet the needs of our diverse community. Included in this process was the superintendent, library media technician, WoW coaches, education services, family and community engagement officers, teachers, counselors, parents, students, and graphic design team members.

After several months of development, the SDWP team narrowed their findings to provide recommendations and the design team landed on six primary design installations that included eleven "missions" or rotations to help students and adults answer three questions: Who am I? Who can I become? How can I get there?

SDWP makes their labor market information (LMI), essential skills rubrics, and MyNextMove career exploration tools available within the Launch Pad to help students and other visitors gain access to valuable tools to help with career exploration activities. A core mission of this community of practice is a dedication to not only serving students within the district, but also the multi-generational family members.

What started as just one Launch Pad will soon be eight new Launch Pads, with new installations planned for the coming school year. This agenda will extend the community of practice across grade levels. Site administrators are tapping existing teachers, library media techs, and counselors to host extension classes and elective periods, and two middle schools now have dedicated career development teachers.

For districts planning to develop a careers-focused community of practice, whether designing a career center or other approach, the local workforce board should be considered in the planning. LMI shared by the board can amplify a program's success by highlighting the careers, pathways, and sectors with the greatest potential job growth. The SDWP team is available to help others plan their approach and the National Association of Workforce Boards can also provide guidance and support for those looking to make the connection.

With the help of ASA, the San Diego Workforce Partnership has provided us with the initial and ongoing support to set up and drive a career center for all ages. The importance of creating this WoW extension and community of practice in middle school is to purposefully advance the integration of career development in our schools. Our work will continue until all students can make informed postsecondary and career pathway choices that lead to gainful employment.

Ed Hidalgo, Chief Innovation and Engagement Officer

Having a bedrock of positive middle grades practices will preemptively set a positive culture on which to build your career exploration programming. These practices, outlined in *The Successful Middle School: This We Believe*, include providing a welcoming, inclusive, and affirming school environment, making certain every student has an adult advocate, and ensuring that policies and practices are student-centered, unbiased, and fairly implemented, to name a few. By grounding your school culture in a whole-child approach, you will have a built-in structure that will serve to enhance the effectiveness of your career exploration programming.

To be successful, your initiative should be guided by a shared vision that is developed by all stakeholders. While that vision is established at the outset, school leadership must seek regular input from each of these groups and frequently communicate their commitment to this work. This feedback may be solicited through quantitative and qualitative means throughout your programming implementation, but it must be authentically reflected on and implemented when appropriate. Communication must also be transparent and regular to build the trust and respect required for good culture to bloom.

By starting your culture building from the planning stages, you improve your chances of success as you implement your program. Some questions to consider as you build a culture of exploration:

1. What assets do our families provide in the home that can support and supplement the exploration programming we are implementing in our school? For example, what skills are students learning at home (bilingual skills, observation of a parent's occupation) that might be leveraged in career exploration programming?
2. How can we leverage our families and community partners to celebrate successes that arise from the program's implementation? For example, a showcase of student's projects may provide an opportunity for stakeholders who might not typically interact to come together to acknowledge the accomplishments of students and share in positive results.
3. What barriers exist to each stakeholder group's full participation, and what proactive steps can we take to

eliminate these impediments? For example, if your staff is hesitant to adopt "one more initiative," how can you as a school leader collaborate with them to ensure that the career exploration programming supports them in their instruction?

What we know to be true is that every school can implement an effective career exploration program, and thereby make an incredibly positive impact on their students and local communities. Leaders can do much to pave the way by engaging stakeholders early and often, identifying and remedying barriers to participation, encouraging students' curiosity and exploration, and giving staff the freedom and support to try new approaches throughout the implementation journey. Program champions should continuously share the value of career exploration and the research that supports its positive impact on student attendance, behaviors, engagement, academic, and long-term success.[1]

Your attitude is infectious, and when you communicate how important and impactful career exploration can be for your students, you set the tone for their success.

NOTES

[1] Balfanz, R. (2009). Putting Middle Grades Students on the Graduation Path: A Policy and Practice Brief. Baltimore, MD: Everyone Graduates Center at Johns Hopkins University, Philadelphia Education Fund, and National Middle School Association. Retrieved on March 12, 2021 from https://www.amle.org/portals/0/pdf/articles/policy_brief_balfanz.pdf

CPSIA information can be obtained
at www.ICGtesting.com
Printed in the USA
JSHW072241050123
35628JS00006B/13